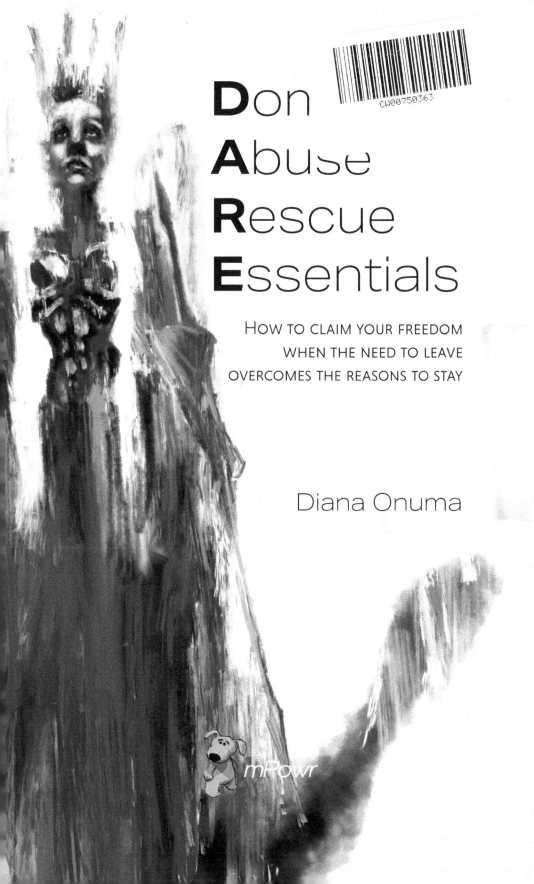

Don **A**buse **R**escue **E**ssentials

HOW TO CLAIM YOUR FREEDOM
WHEN THE NEED TO LEAVE
OVERCOMES THE REASONS TO STAY

Diana Onuma

mPowr

First Published in Great Britain 2019 by mPowr (Publishing) Limited

www.mpowrpublishing.com

A catalogue record for this book is available from the British Library
ISBN – 978-1-907282-92-8

Cover Design and Illustrations by Martyn Pentecost
mPowr Publishing 'Clumpy™' Logo by e-nimation.com
Clumpy™ and the Clumpy™ Logo are trademarks of mPowr Limited

The mPowr Legacy

Every moment of your life has the potential to be more than every moment of your life. As you invest each day into something greater than yourself—lasting longer than your lifetime, influencing those yet to be born—you create a legacy. A legacy that serves others beyond the minutes, hours and years you will ever spend on Earth. The mPowr Publishing mission is to inspire your legacy—to help you create it through the books and media we develop. Every title we publish is more than the sum of its parts, with deeper impact, broader transformation and, at its heart, a legacy that is yours in this moment, right now.

To all the courageous women I have supported, am supporting and will continue to support.

To my family who have supported me to support others—thank you.

In an emergency please call 999.

If you are in immediate danger or need urgent help, please call the 24-hour free National Domestic Violence Helpline on:

0808 2000 247 24.

If you cannot access a phone you can email:

helpline@womensaid.org.uk

Contents

"And the day came when
the risk it took to remain tightly closed in a bud
was more painful than the risk it took to bloom.
This is the element of freedom"

Alicia Keys

INTRODUCTION

You are tired of feeling parts of you disappear every day. You are tired of carrying the heavy, dark burden that gets heavier and darker, day by day. It weighs you down. You feel it in your shoulders, no matter how broad and strong they may be! You feel the niggling pain in your neck and the dull ache in your back.

You want to move on to feel free in your body as well as your mind. You want to make your own decisions. You want to choose what you like and want. You want to move forward. You want to thrive and know what joy feels like.

You are at a point in your life where something has to change. You are in a situation that you feel unsure about how to move away from. You don't know where to start or who to rely on for support. These scenarios are common for someone where you are.

You now feel ready to make fundamental changes to your life. Nobody else can make those changes for you. You are at the crossroads where you want to move away from the unhealthy situation that emotionally and physically drains you.

You will uncover and activate that part of you that will stand up tall, assert your voice and keep you moving forward from pain to peace.

Your wise warrior woman wears *hell no*! heels and a comforting coat of courage to get things done. You will utilise tools to fear less and B.E. more of who you need to start B.E.ing.

You will be inspired and feel compelled to choose a different path forward when you read the real stories of the individuals (names changed) who were where you are right now. The stories of those who chose courage over the captivity of control and abuse.

Welcoming change includes adopting a willingness to think about new attitudes and exploring different ways of doing things. Purposeful power tools provide you with support to fuel you forward away from anxiety. Your can-do attitude will help you to fear less and keep momentum. You will adjust your mindset to plan with purpose and create your own unique vision of freedom.

Once you have begun to claim your power and honour your worth you will feel a thirst for freedom. You will want so much more for yourself. The practical strategies and steps will prepare you to move from helpless to hopeful. To stretch you from shrinking back to standing tall. You will move away from captivity to confidence.

Activate your warrior within. Find your freedom and thrive!

Bodacious Butterflies Boldly Evolving

These women were where you are right now. They will help you understand the real possibilities that sit on the other side of courage.

JODIE

I had finally found my knight in shining armour. He spoiled me with intense, loving attention and gifts. I was the envy of my friends. He was generous with his time, money and affection. He idolised me and I felt like I was the only woman alive!

He supported me in my work, willingly assumed responsibility for my daughter (from a previous relationship) and focused on fulfilling my every need. I had a knack for finding men who were attentive and committed. I was the envy of my friends.

I felt safe with him. In my mind, I felt confident he wouldn't cheat on me. He wouldn't disrespect me. He wouldn't physically hurt me. He was always very protective of me.

However, there was a tipping point. I noticed little things that would make me doubt his genuineness. There were no dramatic signs in this amazing relationship, but these little things niggled me. I had allowed myself to completely fall into trust as well as love with this wonderful man.

I was engrossed in being the apple of my partner's eye and enjoying life. We went on numerous shopping sprees, took many holidays, socialised with all of his friends (not mine). He would drive me to work and collect me. We were always together. The reality of my current situation was becoming clear to me.

To the observers of my life, I was a lucky girl to be with someone like him, someone who worshipped the ground I walked on and put me first in everything.

I began to recognise the subtle dangerous hints of controlling behaviour that had masqueraded itself as a declaration of a deep and everlasting love. I was tired of wearing the mask that portrayed well-being and happiness. Behind the mask I feared the capabilities of this gentle, loving man.

The man who:

- Had secretly threatened my friends to stay away from me
- Had attended my workplace on a number of occasions to change my mind about ending the relationship by threatening to kill himself
- Tried to use my daughter as a weapon in the endless, tiring exchange of words
- Followed me when I went out with my friends
- Sat in his car spying on me at every opportunity
- Forced me to have sex because he needed to connect with me, despite my refusals (I couldn't fight back because my daughter was asleep in the next room)

- Contacted my family members to share his concern about my unstable mental state (because I chose to end the relationship)
- Jumped in front of my car while I was parking outside of my daughter's school

I knew in my heart I had to make some changes so that I could be and feel free. I wanted to walk away from the insistent drives to work, the gentle persuasion not to go out with friends, the mock threats of his ownership of my body, the ever-increasing demand for sex whether I wanted it or not, the over-interest of who I was speaking to at any given time, the jokes about nobody else having me if we ever broke up.

All of my close relationships had become distant. I did not feel comfortable enough confiding in anyone at work for fear of judgement. I felt isolated and alone in my life of illusion. I needed help to remove the mask I was hiding behind.

I was worried about disrupting my daughter's education and security (both emotional and physical). Primarily because I knew I would have to move and had no idea about where I would go.

I had to be smart about what I wanted to do and how I was going to do it. Although I felt immense fear about the changes I wanted to make, I also felt a strange excitement about taking back control of my life. I wanted to leave a positive legacy for my young daughter.

I contacted Diana. We worked together to create a plan that would cover every eventuality. I set the intention to adjust my mindset. I was supported to sow the seeds of change by calling in courage to understand the depth of my reality.

I choose freedom over fear by slipping into my hell no! heels despite my experiences with this man. I chose to rise up! I chose to invest in myself and the possibility of change.

I had felt stuck for a very long time. But the work we did stretched the boundaries of my comfort zone towards freedom. I deliberated and made choices. I changed my mind often. I felt guilt for leaving this seemingly vulnerable man who needed me and idolised me to death, as he often reminded me. This was the natural nurturer in me. My nurturer was yet to be positively empowered, but it was an important item on my accomplishment list.

We worked through the guilt I felt for upheaving my daughter from the material security of the (unhappy) home. Clothes, cars, holidays, designer goods, lovely home—none of it mattered to me when I realised the importance of my personal freedom and the resulting peace that would become my new normality.

With support I pushed through anxiety, turbo-boosted my resilience and really committed to this journey of change. Wherever I was going, I knew it had to be better than where I was.

I was aware of the potential practical and emotional challenges that would present themselves along the way. I was motivated with my hell no! heels to push through the weeds that could threaten my growth from an acorn seed to an oak tree.

With support I felt able to take action and achieve freedom from this stifling, silently controlling chaotic relationship. I felt monumental heights of fear but knew that, to live with peace in my heart and to breathe freely and fully, I had to move through the wall of fear that I felt closing in on me. I knew I had to fear less.

We devised a transitional plan that would ensure as little discomfort and upheaval as possible while allowing me to achieve my intended goals. Armed with my plan of action and guided by my mentor, I felt empowered through each inspired action, step by step, until I was able to physically move away from my situation.

Before I implemented my freedom plan, I explained what was going to happen to my daughter. A few months after staying with a family member I saved enough money to get my own place.

The feeling of victory and freedom I felt when I put the key into what was now my own front door to my own safe space is priceless. It was heart-warming. A memory that still beams from me to this day. It was a soul memory of joy, like nothing I have experienced before.

Diana's note:

The rewards of clear intention coupled with courage and support are profound. I remember the absolute joy I felt for Jodie when she described her pride and excitement at collecting her keys. She committed to doing the work. She activated her inner warrior and achieved success. She was able to gift a positive legacy for herself and her child. You can too.

HANNAH

I grew up in Eastern Europe in a family filled with mistrust and conflict. The relationship between my parents had been volatile and unsettling. My relationship with my parents was turbulent and fault focused.

I felt isolated and very lonely in my country. In my early twenties, I came to the UK, hoping for a better experience. The bright lights and big city life soon dimmed to a faint flicker. The isolation and loneliness had amplified.

Soon after arriving in London, I met my husband who was nearly twenty years my senior.

I now understand, I wanted to fix what was broken and heal what sick in others. I also came to realise I sought the approval of others so that I could feel good about myself. I wanted to be liked, to belong, to be loved. I wanted to feel valued by my husband.

I worked, my husband did not. He controlled the finances. He decided how my earnings would be spent. He directed me to apply for loans and credit cards for his purposes. He told me what I could spend and when. My voice was disregarded and silenced.

I was a sociable, outgoing young woman. My husband was not. He dictated where I could go and how long I was allowed to go for. He told me who I could speak to, when and for how long.

During my first pregnancy I noticed my husband's controlling behaviour towards me intensifying. He had controlled everything. The pregnancy was something he could not control. The abuse worsened.

He hurled insults at me daily about my appearance and my value as a woman and a mother. He undermined me at every opportunity. I had arrived at the critical point in my marriage, where the pain of staying in my situation was far greater than my fear of the unknown.

I instinctively knew that my relationship was not healthy and, after much soul searching, I found the courage to leave. However, I found it difficult to stick to my plan because of a lack of emotional and practical support.

I reluctantly returned to the misery of my marriage. The name calling, constant criticism and accusations became more soul-destroying. The children were subjected to the toxic environment.

I was desperate to get away. I wanted to provide a healthier, loving, peaceful environment for my children, but did not know how to do it without money and family support.

I am a spiritual woman who planted a small seed of faith and hoped with all my heart that I would receive a miracle. I was worried that I would go back to him and the misery if I left again. I became aware of Diana's work supporting people like me as a result of speaking with one of her clients.

I had to be honest with myself about my commitment. I was asked what was different this time? I was so close to getting the help that I needed. I recognised my commitment to myself and the process had to be stronger than before.

I had to be sure of my commitment to move on before I could convince others of my commitment. I knew with certainty that I could not endure the emotional pain any more. I knew with certainty that I would rather face my fear of the unknown than stay in the pain of what was familiar to me.

If I make the same decisions, I will get the same results. Something had to change and I recognised a different approach was needed.

I was encouraged to hold onto my strong faith and use it to propel me through my challenges. As a woman of strong faith this appealed to me because it made me feel secure in my identity as a spiritual woman.

With support and guidance, I learned that my perception of safety and security was housed in a container of abuse and control, diminishing my barely evident voice. The voice I had never properly learned to use. The voice that was constantly quelled throughout my childhood and adolescent years.

The work we did together, helped me to understand that my idea of love came from a deep desire to be needed, accepted and ultimately loved. I realised this desperate need manifested itself in my being compliant and submissive in my relationship.

After our initial session, I knew I was ready to leave and knew with even more certainty I couldn't go back to the despair that had long been my default reality. I was terrified at the thought of going through the leaving process again. I was even more terrified at the thought of what would happen to me if I stayed.

I realised accepting support and guidance would provide me with the opportunity to make the lasting change I deeply desired. We had a robust conversation about my commitment to taking action, particularly in light of the previous incident. We worked together to create strategies to address any vulnerabilities that could undermine the plan.

I attended my appointments with an unshakeable determination to succeed despite feeling gut-wrenching fear. I kept my eye on the outcome I wanted to achieve. It was important that I was supported in a process where I could do the necessary work through the lens of my faith.

We created and activated a comprehensive freedom plan. Inspired actions were prioritised to move me through each stage of my plan with firm faith, commitment and an expectation that nothing less than success would do.

The freedom plan was implemented in stages to allow for adjustment periods and practical flexibilities. Flexibility and self-compassion were key elements here.

On the day I physically moved my belongings I had a lot of physical support to prevent any potential repercussions of the move.

There was an ongoing risk assessment of the environment and the process. The atmosphere was dense with emotion and the taste of freedom lingering. I remember grabbing the last of my bags, getting in the car and I never looked back.

Support strategies were put in place for me and my children. I was allocated a buddy to lean on when I needed to. My support and coaching continued beyond my move, to help me to work through further practical and emotional challenges that presented themselves.

I benefited from support through parenting struggles, contact disputes and the challenges of moving into a new place on a shoe-string budget. But I survived and kept moving forward.

Failure was not an option in my mind. There was too much to lose. I had learned that to put my children first, I had to put myself first by creating a space for us to feel and be safe and emotionally supported.

When I felt confident enough to use the tools I had learned as a result of my coaching and mentoring, I was then ready to fly solo and really be who I discovered I could be.

I am now happily single, living financially independently and enjoying my journey of self-discovery, developing nurturing friendships and reconnecting in a healthy way with my family overseas.

Diana's note:

Hannah had a lot to prove to herself, particularly because she had left the relationship and returned. When she was certain that she wanted to leave for good, she activated unwavering faith. It was important that her belief in her faith was supported as a major part of who she was on her journey. She activated her inner warrior woman on so many levels that she could not fail in her endeavours. The pivotal turning point was when she grabbed her previously packed bags and never looked back.

RANI

I was raised to shoulder a lot of responsibility: for guiding and assisting my younger siblings in every way possible.

My younger sisters were deemed prettier and slimmer than me. More marketable for the purposes of marriage and increasing the overall family's standing in the community. I was invisible and unimportant as a commodity and therefore my family thought it prudent to focus on what they deemed my strengths to be—intelligence and service.

My needs as a woman who desired my own family one day were not acknowledged. My ability to do well in my career was encouraged to enable financial gain which benefited the family for their greater vision of financial advancement and higher social standing.

I had actively learned to put my needs last, I believed this was the only way to live. This was what I was taught. My parents depended upon me from childhood right through to adulthood when my curiosity began to guide me on a journey of self-discovery.

This exciting adventure directed me away from the traditional confines of first responsibility to my family towards an understanding of healthy relationships of mutual respect and unconditional love.

My new discoveries about my life experiences and their intricate lessons stirred up a feeling of unrest in my family's comfort zone. They were unnerved by my excitement and commitment to self-discovery and the new ideas that flowed from this.

I was subjected to physical and emotional abuse by my family for daring to consider that I had needs that deserved be met. I was subjected to endless, unfounded criticism and unbearable bullying from my offended family.

They closed emotional ranks around me to force me to fall into line as taught and as expected. They threatened my safety and freedom by changing the locks to the family home that I paid the bills for.

I was forbidden to speak with or develop a friendship with anyone outside of the family. I was forced to pay all my income to my brother's bank account to curtail any independent action I might want to take.

The turning point arrived when I was removed from my parents' will to demonstrate how dissatisfied the family were with my need to find my own way in the world. I realised my family's motivation was not to invest in my well-being but to maintain coercive control of the role they had attributed to me for their own selfish reasons.

Despite my turmoil, I made a last-ditch attempt to resolve the toxic issues as amicably as possible before seeking help.

My family resented the disruption to what had been the family first status quo imposed upon me. I felt guilty about my new-found knowledge and revelations about myself and my life. I wanted to break free from my inherited role as sacrificer of self in honour of service to my wider family. I wanted to be my own person. I had a right to be my own my person.

I felt torn between my desire to be an independent Muslim woman in my own right and my family's expectations about my role as the go-to person who was responsible for the entire family's needs above her own. I wanted to break free from unfair, entrenched family patterns— not my faith.

I was referred to Diana through another service I was accessing for support. I welcomed the support and guidance I received to work through my conflicted thoughts and emotions. My faith was important to me and I was committed to making positive changes that were aligned with my faith.

I loved my family. But as a result of our focused work together, I came to realise that if they felt genuine love for me there would be greater consideration for me to have and exercise independent living with a healthy respect for my role as a woman. Genuine love would allow me to express my thoughts and opinions. Genuine love would enable them to listen to my thoughts and opinions. Genuine love would encourage strong feelings of worthiness for me as a deserving individual.

I felt a depth of despair ignite in my mind. I wanted to be my own person and to be treated with a healthy respect. I sought Diana's help in my limited freedom from prying eyes and attuned ears. My work with her focused on realistic expectations, personal rules and boundaries and how these fit with the teachings of my faith without undermining its integrity.

We created a freedom and visibility plan with practical and physical action that I knew I could not implement without continued, individually tailored support and encouragement.

I did not want to live in complete isolation. I knew the ostracisation of my family was more than I could cope with. I also knew that to live my own life to the fullest I would have to go through the murky waters of physical and emotional severing of ties, until I was strong enough to B.E. in my power and keep moving forward with a new reality of hope, connection and compassion.

My career was affected by my family's enslavement. I avoided well-deserved career progression opportunities in fear of the family backlash that I would even contemplate having accomplishments in my own right.

I bravely took the decision to remove the daily loyalty mask I metaphorically wore to work. The one that depicted a happy, close-knit, supportive family. I confided in a work colleague who offered me support at work where possible. I was feeling overwhelmed and took some much-needed time off work to give myself time to process what was happening at home and prepare my next steps.

The support I received enabled me to shine the light on the oppression and bullying that I had been subjected to for many years, that worsened following the death of my mother—my only genuine ally in the family.

I was working through grieving the loss of my mother. I was also grieving the loss of relationship with my immediate family members and grieving the lack of relationship I did not have with myself.

The key to working through this grief was to proceed with kindness, patience and compassion for myself while maintaining respect for others and implementing healthy boundaries. The support and guidance I received was gentle but effective to accommodate the process of my grief.

The individualised attention I received encouraged me to grow stronger in my faith in a way that was considerate of my feelings in addition to my family's feelings.

My dilemma was how to create stronger boundaries that represented respect for myself and my intelligent voice rather than continuing to mute my voice, to my detriment, to maintain favour with my family.

For so long I had deprived myself of any meaningful relationships, romantic or otherwise. I learned how to be in a relationship with myself. I was aware my healing would progress when I put myself first. I was conditioned, as most of us are, to put the welfare of others before my own.

As a result of my individualised plan of support, I steadily developed the strength to speak up and implement boundaries. I learned a lot about my unrealised capabilities and strengths and this motivated me to further speak my truth.

I unlearned the imposed behaviour I had inherited and consciously chose to replace it with a positive, loving, compassionate approach to myself and others.

With weekly sessions and the support of monthly group meetings I compiled my freedom plan. The first step was to move away from the hostile family safely. I was supported to navigate practical and realistic stepping stones with care and respectful consideration.

An important aspect of the freedom plan was for me to diligently accumulate finances necessary for me to move from the family home to my own safe space. We explored in great details how much was needed, the various ways the amount could be accumulated and what the transitional timeline would be. I felt excited that I was activating my inner warrior. She was always inside bursting to escape.

With careful planning, a determination to succeed and a group of supportive people in place, all the pieces of the puzzle came together.

I rediscovered my long-forgotten passions and friendships. I moved into new living accommodation and returned to work after a long pause. I found freedom.

Diana's note:

I remember Rani feeling so relieved when she finally got the keys to her own place. She was feeling so trapped in her situation at home with the constant abuse and exclusion. She felt pulled by family expectation, her identity as a modern, independent woman without a voice and her loyalty to always maintain her faith. She employed such determination and compassion. She found freedom by observing her faith unwaveringly and finding her voice to motivate her to succeed with compassion and confidence.

NATASHA

When I first met Tom, a young police officer I wasn't really keen on him. I didn't know why, but something was niggling me about him. I should have paid attention to my inner guidance system. It was alerting me to the hidden dangers to come.

Late one night, Tom came to my home. At the height of one of many, one-sided arguments, Tom followed me around the room shouting and hurling abuse and accusations at me.

I kept moving away to dispel the volatility while trying to hurriedly find a safe escape route. I tried to get him to leave. He threatened to smother our baby (who was sleeping in her cot) with a pillow if I didn't do what I was told.

He cornered me in the kitchen and pulled a knife from the knife block on the countertop. Everything slowed down in my consciousness as he held the blade against my throat.

I froze in that moment. I could feel the coolness of the blade pressing into my throat and saw my life flash before me in slow motion, the fear rapidly rising from the pit of my stomach as he threatened to rape me.

In those life-defining moments something in me shifted. In a heartbeat my thoughts had stopped. I paused, turned slowly and looked into his eyes. I told him to do his best. There was nothing more he could do to hurt me.

As I spoke those words, I felt the strongest I had ever felt. I felt an unexpected peace. And I waited. He dropped the knife and began to smash the furniture while the baby lay in her cot. He left suddenly without a backward glance or his usual deluge of harsh words. His rapid exit filled the room with an eerie peace.

At that moment I knew I had to get as far away as possible from this unpredictable psycho who had become relentless at wearing me down. I had discounted my intuitive feelings of unease too many times. I had allowed myself to be blinded by his charm and intelligence too many times.

A flurry of thoughts was swirling around in my mind. I reflected on our relationship and how I had arrived at this point. We had engaged in a passionate, but short-lived relationship which had ended. The feeling of unease kept coming back stronger each time Tom spoke in a particular tone or shared an opinion that seemed to quash my free and independent spirit.

My every move was being monitored and criticised. The many phone calls were persistent, and I became fearful about not being where I was expected to be, doing what I was expected to be doing.

I had not realised just how much of my former sociable, free-spirited self I had lost. There were a few occasions where I had been walking to my car and Tom had jumped out from nowhere firing questions at me.

I never shared these worrying incidents with anyone close to me. I began to notice articles in magazines about domestic violence and stalking and recognised myself in the stories. I felt disappointed at myself for being so naive and stupid! How could I have missed the signs.

I ended the relationship after a blazing row and felt such a huge relief at what I thought was a lucky escape, until I discovered I was pregnant. Although relieved to reclaim peace of mind, breathing space and feel like my old self again, I was intent on doing the right thing. I eventually told Tom about the pregnancy, after much deliberation and soul searching, for information purposes only.

I didn't know what I was going to do about the pregnancy, but I knew I did not want to reconcile with him. He denied the baby was his. At the height of his tantrum reaction he threatened to cut the baby out of me if I went ahead with the pregnancy. I was thrown back into the turmoil and frightful anxiety I thought I had escaped from.

I had the baby and planned my life as a single parent preparing to complete my university studies. Studying and raising a child proved extremely challenging, but I was determined to do my best and achieve my goals.

Tom eventually found me in my little haven of peace and wanted to become involved with his child. Good intentions were short-lived. He started dictating what I should be doing, when, how and with whom. I became isolated and scared, having very little contact with my family and friends.

I faced a dilemma between being a good, accommodating parent so that our child would have the benefit of two parents in her life and the need to escape the insanity, chaos and fear of this controlling man who exerted his authority at every turn.

I had unwittingly returned to the suffocated, paralysed and fearful reality I had previously experienced. I knew deep within that I had to get away.

I reported that night's incident to the police. Tom disappeared. No further contact was attempted.

I moved away as quickly as possible and focused on getting my life back on track. I was haunted by feelings of guilt about depriving my child of a father.

I discovered some months later that all trace of my police report had vanished as though it never existed. Yet another reminder of the extent a person could extend their control to if they so desired. Tom worked in the police force!

I attended counselling and psychotherapy to address the deep emotions of my experiences. I was on a mission not to be a victim. I didn't want sympathy. I wanted victory. I wanted support. I wanted to move on safely.

I found the support to help me focus on feeling emotionally healthy, asserting myself and building a positive foundation for my daughter by achieving my goals. In my mind this was the best form of recovery from the toxic relationship.

I feel pride in my achievements. I found success despite my circumstances. I was not my circumstance. I rose above and became more than I thought I could be. I worked hard to connect to myself, something I had never really thought about before. I invested in me! I had support and guidance to learn how to look after myself with care and compassion.

Diana's note:

My work with Natasha guided her back to pursuing and achieving her goals so that she could move away from the historic, troubled family legacy she had innocently been born into. She was determined and seriously committed to creating a positive, healthy legacy for her child to inherit. And she did it. She battled with doubt, guilt and worthiness but she kept fearing less. She really owned her wise warrior woman.

PURPOSEFUL POWER TOOLS

Power Quote

THE DISTANCE BETWEEN DREAMS AND REALITY IS ACTION.

Anonymous

Bridge the gap between your dreams and reality by creating a plan and taking realistic action.

Which small, manageable freedom step do you intend to take today?

Power Mantra

I CAN BE WHO I NEED TO BE, TO DO WHAT I NEED TO DO.
I CAN. AND I WILL.

Repeat these words until you feel the impact of them. Feel the power, the motivation and fire of action igniting in your power centre located in your solar plexus.

Power Song

Listen to songs that invoke a firm can-do attitude. Songs that ignite your inner strength and motivate forward movement in a can-do way.

In *I'm a Survivor*, Destiny's Child sing about having a better life, feeling stronger, being richer, wiser, smarter and laughing rather than being sad, now the relationship has ended. Imagine how you would feel if you too were feeling the same benefits? This is a great power song for revving up your warrior woman motivation.

Whitney Houston sings from the depths of her soul about not knowing her own strength in *Didn't Know My Own Strength*. Recall situations where you surprised yourself with your ability to cope in difficult times. Times when you felt you had lost all hope and were wandering alone and confused in the wilderness of isolation and desert of despair.

List three positive actions you took to stand in your strength.

Wise Warrior Woman

Warrior woman wise and strong,

Opportunities for growth embraced in awe of the wonders of life.

Manifesting greatness through inner vision and bold beauty,

Accepting and allowing abundance to flourish.

Never give up, never stay down, victory is your bloodline, wear it with pride.

Warrior woman wise and strong,

Alert for possibilities and regal in hope.

Recalling pure love from long, long ago,

Redressing the balance of victim from old.

Warrior woman wise and strong,

Stands intelligent in bountiful compassion.

Ornate in your glory, adored near and far,

Reclaim your power fiercely and speak your soul's truth.

PURPOSEFUL MINDSET

AWARENESS—COURAGE

AWARENESS

STARK REALITY

There is no masterclass on what a healthy relationship is. There is no masterclass on how to *not* get into a situation where you seek love and fulfilment outside of yourself.

An up-close and personal, intimate dialogue between you and your inner wise self (no matter how deeply buried) is essential. This dialogue is important to point you to your safe space. Your safe space anchors and contains you through the storms of your relationship.

To master the storms you must find a way to connect to the essence of who you are. You have to dig deep and find your inner strength that lays waiting deep inside of you. The quiet, confident voice that offers wisdom. This is the essence of who you are at your core.

You want to end the tireless, circular arguments that wear you down, the constant anxious anticipation of endless accusation and blame, the normality of holding your breath and trying to be two steps ahead of potential incidents.

You have been manipulated so that you have lost your independence or undermined it for lack of self-trust. The incessant and denigrating criticisms diminish your confidence until it furiously fades to a distant point in the sky.

When you are confident in your connection to the essence of who you are, nothing can cause you fear to the point of paralysis or make you feel imprisoned, blocked, trapped, scared of criticism or judgement.

When you are fully connected to the core of who you are, you can and will rise above the storm. You can up-level from the basics of *going* through the storm to *growing* through the storm. The difference is key.

Going through the storm does not guarantee growth to your fullest potential. It just means you survived and will continue to survive. What is it all worth if not to learn about how wonderful, resourceful and powerful you truly are?

Never underestimate your personal power to overcome, understand and rise above the impact of such storms. Growing through the storms will solidify the positives you know, deep down, to be true.

Growing through the storms will enable you to fiercely be the greatest version of yourself.

Connecting with the essence of who you are unlocks your inner warrior woman to stand tall, speak out and breathe from the depths of your soul freely. Sow the seeds of possibility and positivity by allowing yourself to wonder how things could be different.

RECOGNITION

Until you wake in a cold sweat with the familiar feeling of dread in your stomach and your heart pounding so loud it feels like it's going to burst through your ears, you have not arrived at the point in the relationship where you want to change your reality of endless emotional, psychological pain.

Until you find that place where you are desperate for silence to hear segments of your own breath, calm and measured, instead of fraught and frantic fluctuations, you are not ready. Until you acknowledge that place where you feel the torrent waves rise up and threaten to submerge you every time you:

- choose what to wear
- are late coming home from work
- say the wrong thing
- buy the wrong brand of toothpaste
- cook the wrong meal
- are told how you can spend
- are made an example of
- say hello to a familiar passer-by
- hear the secret code word
- gather with family and friends and your smile is painted on and rehearsed a dozen times so as not to elicit suspicion of fear and the evidence of pain behind your mask of domesticity.

Or every time your:

- phone rings
- post arrives
- partner moves in the direction of a particular kitchen drawer

Which of the above indicators apply to you?

What are your other triggers prompting you to change your reality?

You can invest time and energy to fool the outside world. You can try to fool yourself, though I doubt you would succeed for long. Reality has a way of giving you a cold, hard, resounding offensive check-in.

There is voice of wisdom deep inside that prompts you to move. It dares you to dream of a love without the strangled, dark, stifling pain. Whether you listen is another factor.

When your reality is to be seen and not heard. To look good but not too good. To speak only when spoken to. To dumb down rather than share your intelligent opinion.

To shrink back rather than shine. To blend in rather than stand out.

When your reality is to master walking on eggshells to such a degree that you deserve an Olympic gold medal for your attuned technique, accelerated precision and speed.

Something has got to give. Something has to shift. Something has to be ignited.

Your inner wise self is screaming to your highest reverberations, "How much more will you take?"

How much longer will you allow the little light you have left, flickering for survival, to be repeatedly stubbed out?

How many more times will you present your heart to be squashed and trampled on?

How broken do you want to become before you take control back and allow your wounds to heal?

Rewrite your story so that fear is diminished by love, insecurity is eclipsed by courage and loneliness is replaced by connection?

UP-CLOSE AND PERSONAL

You must keep connecting with that quiet, confident, wise, inner voice that speaks volumes when you are still enough and connected enough to hear it. The voice of the warrior woman speaking assertively, seizing opportunities for growth and standing strong in her boundaries. The one who moves forward in her hell no! heels, fearing less.

Get acquainted with your free self, a newer, brighter, high-spec version of yourself. You may struggle to do this at first, if you have never imagined yourself in this way. But you must start somewhere.

Your desire for this has to be stronger than your lust for the latest in-thing. Only, this isn't the latest fashion trend. This is your life. It does not belong to anyone else unless you willingly give it away.

Why would you want to discard something so precious and shiny with raw beauty and untapped potential?

YOUR LEGACY

You were not born from your mother's womb to live a life of control and fear. You have to teach others how to love you. You may not know how if you were not fortunate enough to have such important life lessons shared with you or modelled for you.

You are in control of the legacy you create for your children and your loved ones. What would you like to see unfold for them? Wouldn't you rather they experienced respect, love and freedom, instead of a state of hopelessness, control and fear?

Invest in a legacy rooted in secure, unshakeable foundations and face your weaknesses instead of feeling bad about them.

The gift in facing your weakness is the weight that dissipates when you become aware of and begin to take action to mitigate or alleviate the identified obstacle.

Face your weaknesses to reduce the stronghold it has on you. Allow yourself to explore alternative methods to transform your weaknesses into strengths.

MIRROR IMAGE

Communication is the key to a good relationship. Learning how to speak and how to listen is the foundation. This is equally as important for the relationship you have with yourself.

Where there is an absence of self-connection at a core level, the relationships you attract will reflect that lack of connection back to you. The reflection shows up as feelings or behaviour that mirror your fears and negative beliefs. The change will occur when you intentionally choose to change how you connect to yourself and others.

The lesson is to commit to exploring a gentle, safe, love affair with yourself. Your inner critic may be screaming at you right now, "I couldn't possibly!"

Why not? "I wouldn't know how."

Are you willing to learn? "It never crossed my mind"

Start this love affair now.

What can you do to acknowledge your value?

What will you do to build healthier connections with others?

Allow your outer self to build and develop a healthy relationship with your inner self to create a new and improved version of who you can be.

WORTHINESS

Your self-worth tank is running on low, very near empty. You have to begin to recognise your value as a person. You're not a doormat. You're not stupid. You can achieve things. You do deserve good things to happen to you and for you, despite your past or present circumstances. Rewrite the story and take responsibility for where you want to be.

Don't you deserve better than being criticised for who you speak to or the clothing you wear?

Don't you deserve better than merely coping with life and observing the days and nights blend and weave into one another?

Don't you deserve better than settling for fear that you're not good enough, strong enough, brave enough or supported enough to live freely and wholly?

Don't you deserve better than feeling stuck in something that you know instinctively is not the right relationship for you but the more your friends and loved ones urge you to choose a different path, the more you dig your hell no! heels in and rebel in much the same way as a teen whose parents show concern when they notice from the outside looking in that you are on a slippery slope to sadness? When you feel worthy, you enforce healthy boundaries. You confidently say no without guilt or justification. You take action. You make commitments and stick to them. You connect freely with others.

What are three things that reveal your worth?

What will you do to ensure others recognise your worth?

POSSIBILITY FOR CHANGE

Honouring the capacity to change evokes a fear beyond measure not only in yourself but also your family. Once you decide to take the plunge, to reconfigure your life's blueprint, approach friends and family with compassionate caution.

The reality of their individual stories filter through to what they perceive is their well-intentioned advice or concern. There are some valuable lessons to be gleaned from their experiences. However, remember this is your story. Only you can change the ending.

When you commit to making lasting, positive changes and investing in a legacy of wisdom and growth, you must allow your own thoughts to unfold. You must allow your own analysis of your situation to be the underpinning motivation.

This is a new time for you. You are sowing the seeds of change with each step you choose to take; the preparation has to be right. You are in the driving seat and it is an amazing position to be in.

Take your power back. Reclaim the power you have long forgotten, the power buried deep in your subconscious you never realised you had ownership of. Step into the wise warrior role.

This innate, supreme place within can seem daunting. It is accompanied by pain and discomfort. But, on the other side of the actual or perceived pain of growing into power is the real potential for living peacefully and safely.

You have to grow to know who you are. You have to know who you are to grow on purpose. You have to have a clear vision of what you want. You have to have a purposeful plan to enable your vision to transpire into something realistic and tangible.

Once you understand and accept the possibilities that changing your circumstances can create it is akin to becoming the keen gardener who chooses to have fun designing the perfect landscape garden, step by step.

It takes time to develop—things have to be planted and tended to with care and conscious consideration. The growing starts under the surface, out of sight. The growing starts with your mindset.

As you continue to tend to the soil you will eventually see the young plants, flowers or ornamental grass appearing from the nurtured soil until they shoot out so tall they become healthy flowers, shrubs and reeds, a riot of aromas and colour.

Pace and patience are important features for you as the keen gardener. Developing too fast could cause a perceived readiness that may result in a short-lived bloom.

THE ENERGY OF THOUGHTS

You have been mistreated, are living in extreme fear and subjected to tirades of abuse. There is a part of you that truly believes you are not worthy of a healthy relationship or intimate connection with anyone.

You believe you do not deserve any more than you have experienced to date and there is a strong likelihood that you may be stuck in a repetitive pattern of dysfunctional relationships.

Where is the value in escaping one unhealthy relationship only to fall harder and faster into another? The other person may appear to offer you love without judgement, offer a gentle touch and make you feel like they're contributing to your purpose in life.

Be mindful, with time the facade will begin to crumble. You will find yourself in the same familiar groove of unease and second guessing. You will find yourself in that place where you overspill disappointment.

Essentially you have the same groove but different lyrics. The same product but a different brand! The wolf in sheep's clothing who tuned into your frequency of unworthiness. You prevent this cycle by investing in yourself. Do the work. Find a guide, a supporter and confidant to walk alongside you while you do the work. Prepare the soil ready for planting new seeds.

Change the cycle by changing your thoughts. Your thoughts become your reality, so it is important that you are mindful of what you are thinking in every moment. Elevate your mind to a higher frequency. Raise your expectation of the cards life deals you.

Understand and acknowledge your value by changing the habitual thinking that has contributed to your current reality. When you control your thoughts, you control your reality.

FORWARD FOCUSED

When you arrive at a point of such internal torture that the pain of maintaining the status quo is so great that it overshadows the perceived fears of moving on, you will kick-start the desire to change. It has to be your choice to change the situation.

The chance of success is greater if you willingly decide now is the time to genuinely start to lay the foundations for a different reality. This is the time to prepare the soil for seeds to be planted to enable new growth. This is not a case of overnight success. It is a process that takes careful and considered, comprehensive planning.

Choosing freedom over fear is about choosing to stop the cycle of abuse and control. It is about recognising how to stop. Welcome the wisdom from the peaceful silence of being alone.

You feel lonely when you lose connection with those around you. They fail to understand or see you. You feel isolated or abandoned. Loneliness will be a strong feature of your toxic situation. It is better for you to be alone feeling safe and at peace than lonely and stifled, mute and invisible masquerading in plain sight.

Being alone is a choice to be separate or single. Challenge your fear of being alone by seeing the prospective of being alone as an adventure filled with excitement and curiosity with yourself. Think of being alone as an opportunity to look after yourself with compassion, patience and kindness.

It's better for you to reap the rewards that flow from the value of being peacefully alone. You are able to think your own thoughts, take considered, purposeful action without fear of judgement, needing approval or fear of repercussions.

This is a time to refocus, identify priorities and prepare for a fruitful and faithful future.

EMPOWERING THE NURTURER

The nurturer archetype is the ultimate caregiver. This is the person who says yes to all demands in complete disregard for how their over-commitments and over-loving will impact their own life, health, money, emotions, etc.

The fuel that stokes this fire is the need to please, the need to do good and the need to rescue to your detriment. The nurturer must learn to own their value and the value of those around them by stepping back and redirecting their energy to fill up their tank before they can fill up someone else's.

More importantly the nurturer must pull back and allow others to be responsible for their own actions and thoughts. The nurturer must disengage from the patterns of co-dependency and allow the other person in the relationship the opportunity to become empowered, to embrace responsibility, independence and respect.

What must you go through before you expend all your energy reserves on others?

What will it take for you to recognise and actively respond to your own needs?

Feeling stuck in your need you are enslaved in a lack mentality. How many of these thoughts are familiar?

- I need to be with someone even if they treat me badly
- I need to do this for their approval
- I need to be loved
- I need to help them
- I need to be needed to feel complete

Consider the following:

Who will be with you if you can't be with yourself?

How would life be better if you approved of yourself instead of seeking the approval of others?

Who will love you to the required standard (healthily) if you do not love yourself (healthily) first?

Who will help you if you don't help yourself first?

What would change if you could meet your own needs?

You teach others how to treat you by providing a clear example in how you treat yourself. When you neglect yourself, you teach others how to neglect you. When you choose partners who abuse and control you, on a deeper level you are consenting to this mistreatment by allowing it to continue. When you rely on others to meet your needs instead of taking responsibility for yourself, you give your power away.

RESISTANCE

There is a restrictive cave in you that strongly resists any inkling of change. It feels too remote, uncertain and unsafe. Why on earth would you choose to leave your comfort zone?

Your zone of comfort will never extend to new horizons and stretch you into success if the perimeters are made to look pretty. The value in the stretch would be lost. You have to stretch beyond the familiar to new heights, so you can soar with the eagles.

The idea of change for most invokes feelings of insecurity and lack of control. It can cause a tsunami of panic. What would happen if you chose to be curious about change and fear it less?

Change gifts you a valuable, character-strengthening process. It can magnify your strength and tutor your challenging traits.

When you decide to make changes for the better, the instantaneous inner critic is activated. Its job is to keep you in the illusory confines of your current situation. Your inner critic thinks it is protecting you by trying to prevent you from adventuring forward. It yells familiar phrases to you to hinder you and get you to doubt the validity and success of your new thoughts and actions.

Resistance to changing the norm, breaking away from bondage of fear and unworthiness is a healthy reminder that you are on the right path. When approached with the right mindset, growth and change can be enlightening and educational.

Change can be adventurous and creative. Purposeful planning with clear intentions, patience and pace will reduce the volume of the inner critic to a manageable level, allowing you to forge forward.

PURPOSEFUL POWER TOOLS

Power Quote

WHEN THE AWARENESS OF WHAT IS ACHIEVABLE BRUSHES
YOUR LIFE, YOUR JOURNEY HAS BEGUN

Lori Myers

List the possibilities of what life could become as your awareness grows.

How can your awareness encourage you to choose positive change?

Power Mantra

I ALLOW MY AWARENESS TO INSPIRE ME. I CHOOSE TO BE
POSITIVE AND TAKE INSPIRED ACTION.

Feel the rhythm of this mantra. Repeat it to activate inspiration.

Write down three things that will create change.

Do one each day for the next three days.

Power Song

Think about songs that encourage a different perspective or approach. Listen to lyrics that spur you to think differently or take responsibility for yourself.

I can see clearly now is an uplifter to create a positive mood change for seeing beyond the obstacles and observing the sunshine through the rain.

Grace's version of *You Don't Own Me* is authoritatively performed. These words, repeated, are resoundingly hypnotic. Feel your personal power revolution when you sing, "Don't tell me what to do and don't tell me what to say!" with heartfelt possession.

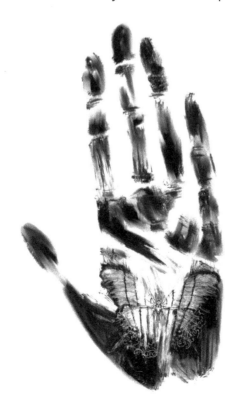

The Trapped Butterfly (Boldly Evolve)

I have loved you through the darkness and the hidden shadows of your pain;

in your feelings of unworthiness and despair

I have tried to break the chains.

The life sentence you escaped from

Brought you breathing space and peace

Allowing you to start rebuilding your life pathway with grace and ease.

The space and freedom while great for a time,

Left you noticing the depths of yourself,

uncovered and exposed, alone inside your shell.

Vulnerability overwhelming,

You fell into a deceptive decline

and sought solace with your old friend,

victim mindset.

Adorned with your coat of **I don't deserve it**

Either that or you walked tall in your warrior woman boots

the pair made for walking in confidence,

only the healthy love path would suffice.

Not the path you are now trapped in

Against your higher-self advice.

You stepped into the Tardis of low energy, masqueraded love

In the hope that you could fill the void of loneliness.

It's masked as I care for you and I love you,

in its apparent gentleness and sway;

The underlying current is destructive and manipulative

buried in darkness and concrete grey.

The spark for self-love legacy,

scattered far into the winds,

Your power and strength,

Your vision and faith,

now deceived by the mask

that cleverly controls.

Stealing every vibrant breath, every sunlit smile,

'Til you're left in a mountain of guilt and shame,

As you expedite your heart's demise

Be strong there is hope in the worn wilderness.

All is not lost.

The fire of faith is fanning its flames,

The angels work effortlessly to repair your broken wings;

To ignite your buried dignity;

To expand your waning motivation.

Power up self-belief, inspire love and gratitude

All to bring you back to SELF.

Back to self for healthy relationships

where exchanges are mutual and respectful.

No hidden dangers lurking;

where love is unconditional,

no neediness or guilt,

where time and space are full of friends and laughter,

no curtailments on socialising or

rules on how to be.

Trapped butterfly cut the cords of self-sabotage and find your way

back to centre

where pure love and soul-nourishing hugs

await you, a safe place for you to breathe and B.E.

Trapped Butterfly no more

COURAGE

SHAME

Shame damages your spirit and keeps you in bondage, shut down to connection and trust. Shame is a weighty burden that falls around you and holds you in a place of suspension between action and inaction. Shame keeps you firmly rooted in the darkness of bullying, blame and criticism.

Shame hides you in the shadow of lying to yourself. Familiar statements such as "It was my fault, I deserved this... I'm a terrible person for getting myself into this situation... No one will want to be with me, I'm damaged goods." To combat this stronghold of shame you must be open to having honest, self-compassionate conversations with people who are in your support team.

These are your buddies, your co-runners who will ensure you complete the race and get to the finish line. They champion your strengths, lovingly nudge you in the direction of your worth and energise you when you are low. They raise you up and fuel your victory fire.

Your support team will help you to understand that your experience is not uncommon, something to be hidden and locked away, something to be minimised and excused. Shame causes you to stay small and silent. Your support team will push you to be the lighthouse and shine bright in the glare of audacity!

GUILT

Guilt leads to a shattered sense of self. Through the lens of honesty, face the reality of your mistakes and accept your part. Take full responsibility from your heart. Be open to learn the lessons that accompany this situation.

Forgive yourself and move on wiser. If you don't know how, ask someone to help you, support you or guide you.

You are conditioned to believe that it is weak to ask for help. You are led to believe that it is not acceptable to be vulnerable. Acknowledging vulnerability is the secret to activating courage and growing in strength.

When you separate yourself from the burden of trying to be ok, you will feel an upward shift of personal power. There is an energetic freedom that pervades you when you choose to remove the mask and be truly present to what you are feeling and why.

Do not continually beat yourself up or become imprisoned in self-hatred. Everyone makes mistakes, the recovery from your error of judgement is dependent on your mindset.

What will you do to avoid feeling guilt and despair about your situation?

How will you approach the situation with self-compassion?

Work from a space of love and compassion to enable you to understand, accept and learn from your mistake with a grace that will benefit your personal growth. This approach will equip you with wisdom and knowledge.

APPROVAL ADDICTION

When you feel bad about yourself and *less than*, you become trapped in a downward spiral of behaviour known as approval addiction to avoid the fear of rejection.

The fear of rejection feels like being unloved or unwanted. It leads you into situations where you are isolated and trying really hard to be loved, liked or accepted. You will seek the acceptance and approval of others to make you feel better about yourself.

When you commit to changing your situation, you will undoubtedly find the beauty of enjoying real safety and true acceptance within yourself. When you stand strong in your power, you do not need the approval of others to feel good about yourself and your life.

You will make decisions for yourself without having to rely on the opinion of others or their permission. When you live in a cycle of approval addiction, your inner compass is muted and your wisdom undermined.

When you maintain the pattern of approval addiction, you lose the connection to your sense of self. If you have never had this connection to yourself, get curious and commit to the practice of loving yourself and building the connection.

Consciously move away from the cycle of isolation, over-giving and care-taking to your detriment. Do it afraid if you need to, but to move through it you must confront the root causes of fear of rejection, fear of abandonment and fear of judgement.

FEAR

Fear keeps you stuck in a prison of torment. As a child you were not taught how to deal with fear. You learned to be scared of fear. You adopted your parents' approach to fear—how to avoid it rather than move through it.

You inadvertently learned how to perpetuate the cycle of fear. Fear is an inherent feature of everyday living. The trick to navigating the daily reality of fear is how you react when fear comes to visit.

The childhood default response to fear or anything remotely associated with fear was: *Stop! Hide! Shrink back! Don't breathe! Don't move! Hopefully it will all disappear and if it doesn't, then just ignore it until it feels like it has disappeared!*

Old memories surface like a cloud of smoke when you read the default fear reactions. Where are the physical reactions in your body at the thought of the default responses to fear?

Is there an intense feeling of a knot in your stomach, a constriction of breath in your chest area or a substantial stifling feeling blocking your throat?

Take a deep breath in from the pit of your stomach all the way up to your heart. Exhale. Release all the tension and angst that you are holding in your body, right now. Exhale until you feel liberated from the shackles of fear.

Your fear is acknowledged loud and clear! There is something of great value when you choose to fear less and do what needs to be done. What would happen if you chose to use the idea of fear as your driving force for change rather than an obstacle to peace?

Fear has to become your motivation instead of your prison. Use the adrenalin to move what appears to be a formidable mountain. Use creativity to fuel the safety trigger that is an inherent signal to break through the fear restrictions lurking in your thoughts.

The idea of fear is often worse than the reality of the situation you attach the fear to. Once you identify the need the fear is feeding, you can implement strategies to meet that need and reduce the overwhelm. The fear that once felt too big, too scary, too tall or too wide, retracts and diminishes to a mere memory.

Reflect upon who you used be before you lost yourself in the relationship that was once happy and safe.

The same relationship that has now become an iron-clad, medieval clasp around your neck restricting your freedom of movement and opinion, suppressing your voice, stifling your breath.

The clasp that keeps you confined in the prison of what used to be your life. Now with that image very much in the forefront of your mind, press the pause button. Take a deep, cleansing, soul-soothing breath.

Imagine a blank canvas. You can be, do or have anything that your heart desires. It is yours for the creating. This is your empty space to fill with freedom thoughts, things and people, if you wish.

Imagine the life you wish you had. Imagine all the possibilities... a clear head, a calm, peaceful environment. Notice the sensations and images that surface now in this moment.

A space where you can laugh or smile without judgement or suspicion. A space where you think independently and make your own decisions.

A space where you can choose how to B.E.: what to do, where to go and when to speak. Who would you be? What would you do? Where would you go?

Step into this alluring space where your B.E.ing, in all its beauty (whether you see the beauty or not), walks through fear. Your B.E.ing sees past the illusions and the hopelessness.

You have to want to change your reality with a mighty momentum that fuels a brave determination, an unwavering will, a deep-rooted, faith-filled vision, and a bedrock of conscious connection to others for soul-soothing support.

This mighty momentum is found when you make a heart-based, soul-centred promise to yourself—that hidden part of yourself that yearns for more. That part of you that inherently knows there is hope and freedom dancing in the distance. That part of you that secretly knows there is a better way.

The shift happens when you acknowledge that the pain of staying where you are is far greater than the fear of the unknown. The shift occurs when the pain of staying in the relationship that strangles the life force from you is far greater than the fear of uncertainty about who you could be if you choose to walk away.

This process honours yourself and drowns out self-opined weaknesses whispered by your inner critic and that engages a self-denigration onslaught.

COMPASSION

Compassion is vital to cultivate growth and healing for you, your situation and those around you. It is all too easy to demonstrate compassion for others. It is often more of a challenge to indulge in self-compassion.

Think of a time you heard a loved one or friend berating themselves, harshly judging themselves for a decision made or action taken, and you felt they were not being fair to themselves.

Now think of a time when you berated yourself and harshly judged yourself and when challenged explained that your situation was different. What makes one situation different to the other? You more readily demonstrate a loving and caring nature towards another than you would yourself.

This indicates a lack of compassion for self, amongst other things. You are seldom taught to shower yourself with love and kindness. In fact, many cultures encourage putting others before yourself.

You risk being labelled selfish or self-centred if you attempt to put your needs first. Your heart space and soul existence require you to care of yourself first. Be kind. Be gentle. Be forgiving. Be understanding. All of these qualities must be invested in for a stronger sense of self to be materialised.

Make self-compassion the rule, rather than the exception.

ALLOWING

You have to be willing to change and seek transformation on a deeper, heart level. Tune into the deeper feelings that reside in your heart. Listen to your intuitive prompts. Identify your motivation and let that be your driving force that will propel you to a freedom path of peace.

Give yourself permission to be uncomfortable through your heart and soul growth. When a woman chooses to have a baby, she will hear of the pain and discomfort of labour and delivery.

Despite the varying descriptions of labour, she will ultimately prepare herself mentally and physically for the experience. She will start to think about coping strategies, pain relief and support in the room when the time comes.

As a result of the information gleaned, she is now prepared and endures the path of childbirth because she knows that the outcome will provide her with a baby. The pain becomes a distant memory disappearing from her awareness.

The purpose and result of her childbirth experience far outweighs the level of pain and discomfort, worry and anxiety she may have experienced along the way. At the point the woman set the intention to proceed along this path she was giving herself permission to experience the short-term pain for the long-term gain. The positives far exceeded the negatives.

Allow yourself to be and feel your vulnerability. Your inner strength will surface and guide you to soul-nourishing safety. There is resounding strength in asking for help or outwardly expressing concerns to every last detail. Take responsibility for finding the resources and support required to help you achieve success.

The alternative is to perpetuate the cycle of victim mentality which dictates that everything is hopeless and there are no options or sufficient help available. Victim mentality keeps you stuck where you are; in the shadows without the light of hope or the water of wisdom, to move you to a better way of being and feeling.

Allow fearful feelings, discomfort and pain to release, dissolve and transform. Removing yourself from this situation is the first step to exercising your personal power. You will raise your self-esteem. Find your voice and ask for what you want and need from those around you. Enter a gentle but firm dialogue with yourself to firmly plant fertile emotional seeds for growth.

ACCEPTANCE

Identify where you are and how you came to be here with a view to crafting a new and improved version of you, with the very necessary addition of boundaries. What do you choose to do with the pain you have endured? Will you use it for grievance or positive purpose?

Possibility starts with accepting the reality of where you are in life at this moment. Be honest and vulnerable. See with your senses and feel with your inner compass the scale of your unhappiness, the debts of your fears, the yearning of your soul.

Choose to change your reality. It starts with you. Just as the acorn grows into a mighty oak tree so too can you rewrite your story, change entrenched habits and escape the limitation you have unconsciously surrounded yourself with.

If you were wide awake in a dream of your life as it is now, step into your warrior boots and change your future. Make conscious, positive choices to align you to the path you were destined to flourish on.

RESILIENCE

What will you do to pick yourself up, dust yourself off and keep going? You must feel with confidence that you will do this no matter what presents itself. You must know where you are going and how you will get to your destination.

Resilience is the backbone of your success in this process. You will have to deal with disappointment, conflict and, most certainly, fear. You dig deep and find every ounce of inner strength to keep moving forward, little by little, step by step. Keep taking progressive steps and stay focused on what you want to achieve, you cannot fail. Jodie, Hannah, Rani and Natasha could not have succeeded without resilience.

Develop your emotional stamina to build resilience. It works like a muscle. You have to exercise it for it to become stronger. Become aware of the triggers that send you in a downward emotional spiral and learn coping strategies for them.

Avoid taking things personally. This is not the time to sit in your sensitivity. Be objective in your assessment of a situation. Observe your emotions as they surface instead of instantly attaching them to a comment or circumstance. Armour up and stand tall. Walk in faith, not fear.

It is resilience and a clear, comprehensive freedom plan that will walk you through the doorway of doubt and the forest of fear. You have the resilience muscle. You are using it in your current situation. You have endured so much pain and despair and yet you pick yourself up, dust yourself off and keep going.

You pick yourself up even when you have no fight left in you. You pick yourself up when you have no voice, no vision, no choice. You are exercising the resilience muscle. You need to own it and use it to benefit you in a more empowering way. Pull on the warrior woman boots and step to it!

ANXIETY

Your faithful friend, anxiety, will fight tooth and nail to stay by your side, whispering its versions of sweet surrender to its partner in crime, resistance. It is great to be loved and connected, but seasons change and cycles end. If you continue to do what you have done up to this point, then the results will be the same.

You will be on this perpetual merry-go-round of toxicity and pain. To release the stronghold that anxiety will undoubtedly attempt to retain, you have to have a plan. This must be a clear, carefully considered, bite-sized, step-by-step plan of action.

Your plan must be accompanied by fear-resistant empowerment tools alongside a super, soul-nourishing team of supporters to really hold a heartfelt, healing space for you. This is a safe and boundaried support system for you to work within.

Your healing space is an emotionally supportive and equally emotionally accountable support system for you to unfold in and find your voice to speak up.

Your supporters must be committed to your personal growth. They will have your back. They will dry your tears. They will walk every step with you and give you constant encouragement to help you feel secure to move forward.

Be present in each moment. Do not worry about what has happened or what could happen. Purposeful planning has its place. However, your old friend *anxiety* needs constant reassurance to reduce its influence upon you.

FEELING STUCK

Feeling stuck is a state of mind. Indecision is a state of mind. Be aware that when you decide not to make a decision or take action, you are making a choice to maintain the status quo and stay stuck!

If you find you are moving through life in circles much like the twirly red and white swirls emblazoned on the oversized seaside lolly, you will arrive at a point (if you are not there already) where you will experience such compelling feelings of enough overflow that you will intentionally and internally shift your thoughts to creating something better.

When you hit rock bottom, the only way is up; no matter how slow the pace, heavy the load or high the wall. Mountains can be climbed. You require the right tools for the climb. You must focus on the outcome. Focus on how best to climb to the top.

Plant the seed of success in your mind and allow it to become deeply rooted. Picture the feeling of achievement when you are standing on the mountaintop reflecting on the triumph of your climb. Feel the pride of your success. Try on the coat of courage.

To shed the heaviness of feeling stuck, make a commitment to flip the switch. Consciously focus on what you want. Do not stress about how this will happen. Take things in stages to avoid overwhelm.

Give yourself permission to think of a life free of control, fear, isolation and judgement. Dive into your imagination superpower.

EMBRACING POSSIBILITIES

You hold an acorn of belief that you need to cultivate with appropriate support to firmly take root and grow into a mighty oak tree. The oak tree will not break at ferocious winds nor wane at thundering storms. You will find strategies that move you through the winds of change and thunder of life storms.

The oak tree knows and has confidence in its strength to withstand whatever chaos blows because of her quiet resolve and deep-rooted strength. Your strength will increase with every positive action you take.

The mighty oak has its roots extended securely into the earth with surface space to breathe and B.E. This is where you aspire to be. Space to finally breathe and B.E.

Develop a hopeful mindset and practise perseverance. If you struggle to believe in changing your circumstance, think about your situation in stages. Adopt a belief that is one stage away from what you wish you could believe. When you are comfortable at that stage, identify what needs to be in place for you to move your belief one stage up to where your situation is. Momentum will flow and increase positive belief. You will begin to see possibilities.

WILLINGNESS

You have to be willing to change your reality. Be brutally honest about where you are in this moment and what you intend to do about it. At this point don't worry about the *how*. You have to make a commitment to yourself and embrace the risk as an exciting adventure—fresh soil to plant seeds for new growth!

You have to be willing to fear less and grow forward.

B.E. willing to

- exercise faith
- have a big vision
- replace old behaviours with new ones
- be kind to yourself and show outrageous compassion
- let go of things, people, places or activities that no longer serve you

FAITH

Miracles happen when you take a giant leap of faith. The universe responds to your solid intention to positively shift your mindset. Take bold, self-supporting action to open up doorways and allow your necessary path to unfold step by step. Hannah believed in the power of faith and opportunities unfolded. You have to find that faith place in you.

You must trust and believe in a mighty, unseen power bigger than you. All you need is a tiny, mustard-seed-sized belief that good things are in store for you. You must believe that you deserve better and allow good things to come to you and work for your benefit.

Faith is love based and focuses on possibilities. Fear is pain based and draws your attention to limitations and insecurities. The destructive power in your circumstance does not come from a healthy love base. The person you want to move away from has had their own fear-based experience.

You can help them by believing in and acting on a love-based faith power that removes you from their fear pit. They will have to address the void that is left. That is their journey, not yours! Focus on your life. Focus on your needs. Focus on your worth.

Walking the faith path empowers you to realise the extent of the expansive abundance waiting to be claimed. It is like winning the lottery and not presenting your ticket for your rightly deserved winnings.

Walking the fear path is like walking as the shackled prisoner who has been freed but is too scared to live freely. Avoid feeling regret at missed opportunities and replace the mountain of fear with the higher mountain of faith.

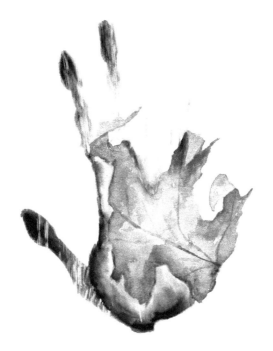

PURPOSEFUL POWER TOOLS

Power Quote

I LEARNED THAT COURAGE WAS NOT THE ABSENCE OF FEAR, BUT THE TRIUMPH OVER IT. THE BRAVE MAN IS NOT HE WHO DOES NOT FEEL AFRAID, BUT HE WHO CONQUERS THAT FEAR.

Nelson Mandela

Move through the fear despite how scared you may feel. The moment you face your fear, real or perceived, its power diminishes. Which fear will you move through first?

Power Mantra

Repeat this power mantra to keep your momentum going. Start with a slow pace and pick up the power behind the words each time you repeat it.

Power Song

Listen to songs that ignite a ferocious attitude of courage. Find songs that speak to your inner strength and motivate forward movement fearlessly.

Katy Perry powerfully asserts her champion spirit and warns the other person to get ready "'Cause she's had enough," in the triumphant song, *Roar*. Notice how you feel when you listen to those lyrics about getting up despite being held down.

Sia's *Titanium* echoes the determination described in *Roar*... being shot down, but getting up. This is a powerful, motivating song to build up courage and resilience.

Where are you feeling the force of emotion as you listen to the melody and lyrics? In your stomach? In your heart? Our bodies are wise and communicate our soul's honesty through physical indicators in our body. Turn your attention to the internal indicators of your external issues.

ESSENCE OF COURAGE

Face the waves of terror and fear fermenting all around,

Honour the stillness and wisdom of silence that surmounts the tirade and obliterates the waves.

Stand tall in the shadows, be vibrantly bright.

Illuminate the depths of darkness with the light of love and firm resolve.

Nurture the contours of courage, building layer upon layer,

Breath after breath.

Hold hope in your heart to banish the fear

Take hold of fierce vision, triumph is near.

Activate your freedom plan with purpose and pride,

Unleash inspired self-love

Devoid of all judgement.

Share forgiveness fully and a wealth of worth,

Fill up your love tank with heart-centred hope

Fear-giants defeated, the path ahead cleared.

Celebrate your warrior wisdom, vision and faith

Dance with delight to your tune of victory

You have overcome, risen up,

Shine bright, fly free.

PURPOSEFUL
PRACTICALITIES

Purposeful Planning

Bring your awareness to the shift you are feeling. Notice the faith and courage mindsets that have been activated. What will you do when the pain of staying where you are is far greater than the pain of moving into the unknown?

This is a transformational point despite the doubts and fears swimming around in your mind. It is time to create your new reality. There are a number of things you will have to think about.

You will tie up loose ends by pruning back the weeds to allow healthy growth in your fertile mindset.

You may have little to untangle, a little snip here and there and you are ready. Or you may have entwined vines, leaves, thorns. Do not panic. You will disentangle the strands and take a bird's-eye view of potential issues.

There may be legal matters, housing matters, family matters, child related matters, parenting matters, financial matters. Your natural reaction is to pull away from some of these topics, but they are all relevant to healthy independent growth, freedom and peace of mind.

Your safety is paramount so ponder the practicalities within the context of the risk of harm to you or your loved ones.

There is a lot think about and work through so be aware of overwhelm, fear and doubt creeping in. This is perfectly normal. When you are forewarned and forearmed with an understanding that it is normal for these feelings to surface and know the step-by-step plan to follow, you will be better equipped to adapt.

Observe the variety of feelings that surface. They are a natural response to you uncovering the hidden depths of an emotional resilience you never knew you had.

Allow the feelings to surface and move on, like a quiet stream gently trickling over the random rocks until it is no longer in sight.

It is important for your healing that you acknowledge and honour every emotion that surfaces, understand it in its context and then release it. It will not serve you to hold on to or ignore such feelings. They will only persist, potentially increasing your fear factor.

Your plan must contain step-by-step action and include a comprehensive consideration of your values. That plan must reflect the outcome you want to achieve.

There are a number of aspects that you have to consider. Start with the most common issues that can arise following the end of an unhealthy relationship.

Trust the mindset shifts you have made. Forge forward to freedom with courage and wisdom.

Simple Success Steps:

- Breathe... when it all feels too much. Take a moment to be still. Take a moment to breathe.
- Find a buddy who will support you and hold you accountable during this time of transition.
- Brainstorm actual and potential practical issues you may have to address in this transition.
- Create two lists for these issues. One for time-sensitive tasks/issues. The other for financially dependent tasks/issues.
- Undertake a strengths and weakness audit to allow you to identify where you need help and support the most.

- Find organisations that can assist you with legal or financial issues.
- Get organised. You will be making lots of lists, phone calls, enquiries. It is important you have a system for finding the information. Use notebooks and folders to keep paperwork safe and organised.

Unwanted Behaviour

Prepare yourself for the possibility of unwelcome, unkind, concerning or even criminal behaviour from the person you are walking away from.

There are so many different reactions that could surface during the transition period that follows the conclusion of the relationship. The aim here is to present you with the range of possible scenarios rather than instil fear.

You are in the best position to anticipate how the other person will react to the relationship ending. Where there has been serious physical violence or psychological reaction you must ensure your safety is paramount and protected.

You will need careful safeguarding measures in place. Have a robust support system and a coherent ongoing protection plan in place.

The cycle of grief and loss illustrates the common emotional stages of typical reactions: shock, denial, anger, blame, resistance, bargaining, depression, concluding in acceptance and recovery.

The behaviour that creates a cause for concern is when the other person begins to:

- continuously contact you or approach you
- threaten you directly or gets someone else to threaten you
- physically harm you or attempts to harm you
- damage your property

Such behaviour can seriously impact your emotional, psychological, financial and physical well-being and those who care for you or who you care for. This is the moment for the warrior in you to stand strong and tall. Your equally strong and tall support team will drive you to move mountains and push through doubt.

Dealing with unwanted attention or behaviour is like holding steadfast in the midst of a category five hurricane. You know it is coming, you take all necessary precautions for safety. You find shelter during the storm.

You know it may wreak destruction. With foresight and safety measures in place you will feel confident that once the storm has moved on or diminished you will still be here to tell the tale. Your warrior coat of courage and the sword of faith will serve you well.

The unwanted behaviour may sound extreme to you, but the reality is sometimes your relationship can start with simple beginnings and end up turning into a nightmare of events that can spiral out of control. Anticipating the other person's behaviour allows you to have necessary strategies to reduce your emotional stress and overwhelm.

Laying the foundations—identifying what you need to do, who you need to be and what you need to have in place—can make all the difference to riding the storm with wings of steel or feathers of dust.

Preparation and support are key. A mindset masterclass is compulsory. In some circumstances there is nothing to expect or anticipate. In other circumstances there will be a mental and physical tug of war for the person with the most endurance.

Simple Success Steps:

- Anticipate a range of reactions and have considered responses or practical measures in place for these reactions.
- Organise a small group of robust, reliable individuals who can ride the storm with you by providing the support you need.
- Think about the emotional and physical boundaries that must be in place to ensure a successful outcome.
- Review your privacy settings on your phone, tablet and computer to protect your location and online identity.
- Consider changing your telephone number and email address.
- Seek professional help if you feel at serious risk of harm.

Cutting The Ties That Bind

As you grow from acorn to oak, pull up the withered roots and weeds. Remove the

dis-eased, dried foliage that will impact the effective nourishment of the other growing vines and branches and stunt the growth of your flourishing tree.

Moving away or finding a new home is often the first action that needs to be addressed. This can be the most challenging decision to make. Your home represents your safety and it is a place where you can be yourselves to the ignorance of the outside world. Alternatively, your home may represent a place of fear where terror and abuse prevail. Let the memory of fear and terror motivate your move to a place of safety.

Your home is where your comforts, memories (happy and sad) and rituals exist to the exclusion of those outside. Your home is your privacy. Approach the move through the lens of adventure and necessity.

Wipe the slate clean. A blank canvas to design a new landscape. To bring brighter colours, more warmth to your garden of life. You choose which seeds to sow. You have the power.

Moving can be simple or complex depending upon a range of factors. Sit down with someone you trust to be honest, sensible and solution-focused. Brainstorm housing choices that may apply to your situation.

For example, if you live in privately rented accommodation and both your name and your partner's name are on the tenancy agreement, is there a possibility that your landlord will change the tenancy into your name only?

If you live in your partner's home and want to leave immediately, do you have somewhere that you can stay safely for a temporary period? This helps you gather your thoughts and think about your next steps without being bothered by your partner.

Be creative with your choices and remember nothing has to be a permanent decision right now. This is why it is so important to have a clear, realistic but flexible plan for moving on. Avoid overwhelm by planning your next steps as small, manageable tasks.

Simple Success Steps:

- Practise daily gratitude to provide a positive focus during what is often an emotionally and physically overwhelming time
- Brainstorm all accommodation options. List everything that comes to mind, no matter how unrealistic it may seem
- Work through each option to reality-test the feasibility and reasonableness of each viable option. Consider factors such

as cost, location, proximity to school, work, friends and family

- Create a contingency plan based on the information you have. Accept you may have to work to a transitional arrangement where finances or housing options are limited
- Think about how you can protect your privacy now, during your moving phase and when you have settled into your new home
- Reward yourself for your efforts. Celebrate every action you complete

Children

Navigating a move towards safety and freedom where children will be affected can be a delicate and gut-wrenching exercise. You will feel torn between what you need and want for your own safety and sanity, and what your child wants or thinks he\she wants (depending on their age and their emotional capacity).

The emotional recovery of children often depends upon the quality of the parental relationship post break-up. If separating parents can disengage from their own individual emotional wounds and focus on positive communication and cooperative, practical parenting the emotional harm to the children can be substantially reduced.

A child has a right to spend time with each parent as long he/she is not at risk of serious harm. In circumstances where one parent has physically harmed the other, there are protective measures that can be put in place to ensure the child can spend time with that parent safely, despite the harmful behaviour.

Boundaries are a vital ingredient for success between parents who separate. Some boundaries may have to extend to legal measures should the circumstances warrant it.

When feelings of guilt surface there may be a temptation to acquiesce to keep the peace. Give serious considerations to your motivations for encouraging or restricting contact. There is a danger that the focus on parental needs supersede the child's needs.

As a parent you have a responsibility to keep your child safe and protect them from harm. Staying in an abusive relationship or repeatedly entering into such relationships with your child can cause harm to your child that could, in a worst-case scenario, result in social services' involvement.

It is vital that you move away from abusive or unhealthy situations to ensure the emotional and physical well-being of yourself and your child. Children do not have to witness abuse or violence to be affected by it. The tipping point is that you are affected, whether you realise it or not.

If you fail to address the situation it will pervade through every facet of your emotional health, creating a ripple effect of emotional imbalance for your child. What is the legacy you wish to hand to your child?

If you were in the position that your child now finds him/herself in, what do you wish your parents would have done about the situation?

How would you feel about your life now, had those steps been taken?

What might you have achieved if you had not been exposed to that situation?

Simple Success Steps:

- Identify the motivation for your view about whether your child should spend time with the other parent
- Accept responsibility for your own emotions and be honest about the origin of your concerns
- Offer a considered response rather than rash reaction to a

request for contact between your child and the other person

- When in doubt seek assistance from an impartial, independent person
- Commit to communicating with your children rather than communicating about them. Children feel and see what is occurring and deserve to be informed about things that affect them. Use age-appropriate language to keep them updated
- Pause and take a breath

Finances

Consider how you will support yourself (and your children if applicable). If you are financially dependent upon the person you are seeking to leave, start thinking about how you can become independent. It may be something that will have to happen in stages.

The reality is you may have to accept that your standard of living will alter in the interim and perhaps permanently for the future. Financial co-dependency is one of the tightest dis-eased vines of limitation you can place around yourself as a reason to stay in a soul-destroying relationship.

When you love yourself enough, you wake up to a horizon of hope. You start climbing the mountain of possibility. You find a pathway through the obstacles, real or perceived.

Place a higher value on who you are on the inside rather than who you are trying to be on the outside. Decisions based on fear create consequences made from fear.

Simple Success Steps:

- Brainstorm creative ways to raise and accumulate money

regardless of the amount. If you start putting the odd coin in a hidden jar, you will be amazed at how quickly the money jar can fill up. This will be a useful amount to contribute to your freedom fund.

- Declutter. Identify items in good condition and make arrangements to sell them.
- Open a secret bank account and every time you get paid or receive money take a small percentage and allow it to quietly grow in the background.
- Research exactly how much money you will need to meet the immediate expenses of moving if that's what you plan to do.
- Undertake a budget of your likely living expenses in your new reality.
- Check entitlement to benefits, loans or grant payments for somebody moving into your new reality.

Emotional Support

The support of your family and friends is crucial as part of your healing process. However, seeking support from an independent source will be of immense value to you when you feel you have exhausted all family and friend options.

Support from an independent source (someone without emotional attachment to your situation) allows you to receive neutral and objectively productive assistance. The type of support you may require is based upon your experiences in the relationship.

If you have suffered trauma or extreme physical or emotional abuse you may want to consider psychotherapy or trauma counselling. If you suffer with anxiety or panic attacks you may wish to consider cognitive behavioural therapy or cognitive behavioural hypnotherapy. There are a range of interventions that may be useful.

If your experience of the relationship has caused you to become isolated and low in confidence, consider joining a holistic healing programme that will address your concerns in totality. Look for a programme that will provide a safe, nurturing space in which to break down and remove the old patterns.

When you feel like you have lost your identity and mojo, it helps to recover from the relationship by connecting with others who share the same or similar experiences. There is a tapestry of wealthy wisdom that transpires when a group come together to work towards rediscovering their identity and reactivating their mojo.

There is a magnitude of scope to create a fresh vision of hope and possibility for yourself–this metaphorically fertile, new landscape of *being* by choice. You choose who you are. You are not defined by your relationship experience. You become who you are growing into.

Simple Success Steps:

- Arrange quiet, focused time to reflect on your experiences throughout the relationship and journal the feelings and emotions that surface.
- Notice what types of behaviour trigger emotional responses from you.
- Notice how you tend to react when a relationship ends. What measures have to be present to keep you strong and independent?
- Be honest about whether you think you need independent or professional support through your healing process.
- Find a new hobby or activity to support your moving-on mindset and increase your confidence.
- Speak with your buddy about helping you to identify healthy boundaries.

Boundaries

One of the proven keys to success at this stage is having firm boundaries in place. This is often an area of monumental neglect.

If you struggle with boundaries you may fear being judged for being selfish, mean, inconsiderate. You may fear being rejected and feeling alone, isolated and unsupported.

Guilt and worthiness issues will present themselves. These are all common fears that will continue to pop up and tap you on the shoulder at times when you feel confident that you have indeed addressed the issue.

The illusory potential drama is often a test of faith stretching you to solidify your commitment to growth. The drama is a prompt for you to recognise and reflect upon the evidence of your progress so far on your freedom journey. The purpose of this intervention is for you to acknowledge and take ownership of the reality and scale of your growth.

Your growth will flow from your positive, fear less mindset adjustment. And the benefit of accessing appropriate support to guide you through the darker pathways of your experience firmly embeds itself in your thoughts.

Find a mentor, coach or attend personal development workshops. Focus on accessing specific support that will help you understand how to create boundaries and support you in honouring and enforcing them.

When you commit to stepping into your power and honouring your boundaries, the people who take advantage of your kindness, undermine your confidence or crush your vulnerability will protest the loudest.

They are the people who will feel affronted at your audacity to boldly evolve and will find every opportunity to make you feel guilt or shame. It is crucial you invest in your mindset makeover toolkit and speak your truth. Stand strong in the midst of the storm.

There will be a firm resistance to change. When you change, others around you will have to change in response to the changes you make. The question is will they follow your lead and adapt positively?

Or will they choose the familiar, overgrown, weed-riddled path of pain and negativity because the idea of change imprisons them in their own forest of fear?

You will experience relationship dynamics shift. You will have doubts about yourself and your decision to change. Stand strong in the midst of the storm. Take a deep breath.

You will notice friendships fade away because you are now different. And that's ok. You are evolving into the new you! New and improved. Stronger and more confident. Listened to and seen. Validated and vibrant. Wise Warrior Woman. You rock! You are becoming the growth goddess.

The tree cannot grow without the rain. Rain can make us feel cold and wet. Rain can refresh us and awaken us. Change can bring initial discomfort, but it acts as the rain does.

Change can catapult us to greater heights by steering us to step out of the comfort of what is known to us and embrace the adventure and possibilities. Alternatively change can cause us to stand still, shrink back and hide: confining us to stress, fear and hopelessness. Which path would you rather be walking?

Simple Success Steps:

- List six respect rules (boundaries) you want to enforce.
- Display (paint them, type them, cut them out and stick them on a board) your rules where you can see them at every opportunity.
- Recognise and write down six ways you can honour the boundaries of the other person.
- Identify poor behaviour you may have demonstrated and take responsibility for it.
- Practise stating your boundaries out loud.
- Review your boundaries every few months to make sure they are still valid.

PURPOSEFUL POWER TOOLS

Power Quote

BOUNDARIES ARE NOT WALLS, THEY ARE THE GATES AND FENCES THAT ALLOW YOU TO ENJOY THE BEAUTY OF YOUR OWN GARDEN.

Lydia H. Hall

Boundaries inform others about your standard of self-respect and self-love. The absence of boundaries is an open doorway for neglect and abuse to enter. Create healthy boundaries to teach others how to enjoy a healthy connection with you.

Power Mantra

I AM THANKFUL THAT MY NEEDS ARE ALWAYS MET.

Repeat this power mantra three times before you start your day.

Set a clear intention in your belief that help and support is always available to you. The help may not come in the way you might expect it or from the person you would expect it from. But help and support will always show up.

Power Song

When Andra Day sings about rising up like the day, rising up unafraid, imagine the power behind the words in much the same way the dawn mist clears to reveal the presence of a panorama of majestic mountains.

Mountains represent transformation. See yourself climbing your transformation mountain. Shout from the top of its magnificence. What is the next inspired action step you are now ready to take?

An Alicia Keys interlude entitled *The Element of Freedom* is the perfect illustration for this section. "And the day came when the risk it took to remain tightly closed in a bud was more painful than the risk it took to bloom. This is the element of freedom."

Accept what is and break through your obstacles with determination. Bring on the warrior! Step into freedom!

Freedom

I made it...

through the darkest nights

the longest days

the drought of tears

the lack of breath

I accept my conscious choice to replace...

the oppressive old with the nurturing new

the familiar pain with powerful peace

the overwhelm with measured steps of inspiration and purpose

the despairing doubt with furious faith

I release...

the repetitive patterns

the ties that bind

the lurking fears

the need to please

the strongholds of my mind

I value...

Peace

Purpose and passion

Personal power

All that is healthy and good for my soul

I value...

My voice

My space

My life

My heart

I value

My right to be free

I B.E. to be ME

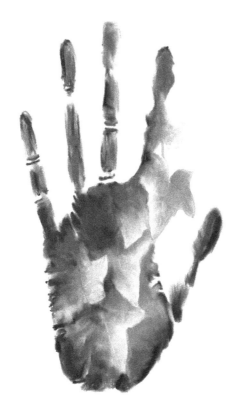

THE JOURNEY BEGINS...

Trapped Butterfly no more.

Exhale!

Dance!

Own who you are!

Walk tall with the Coat of Courage,

Stride strong with the Warrior Boots,

Fear Less.

Grow the acorn inner love,

Bring the rain of outer radiance.

Speak up.

Shout out.

Sing loud.

Move freely.

Fear less.

Trapped Butterfly no more.

Exhale!

Dance!

B.E. who you are!

Change is a constant feature of life. You cannot prevent it. You may delay it, but it will keep presenting itself to you.

Change is part of your soul journey of evolution to learn life lessons and grow. If you resist, you find yourself back in the same spot, issue or circumstance until you surrender to the call and step into becoming who you are with faith instead of fear.

Choose to rise up.

Choose to step into your hell no! heels.

Take back your power.

Activate your inner warrior woman and thrive!

What will your next step to freedom be?

APPENDIX

SPIRITUAL POWER TOOLS

How to use the stones

Ensure the crystal is cleansed before use. Set the intention to experience the benefit of the crystal you choose. Meditate with the stone in your hand, keep the stone in your pocket or bag or place on a surface near you.

How to use the essence

Set the intention to experience the benefit of the oil you choose. Apply on your pulse points or inhale by putting a drop in your palms, rubbing together and taking three deep inhalation breaths. Alternatively, diffuse the oil in a diffuser.

AWARENESS

Power Stone

Garnet strengthens the survival instinct and encourages hope. This stone also helps you to let go of those things that no longer serve you.

Hematite boosts self-esteem, enhances willpower and increases confidence.

Power Essence

Juniper berry helps to break the ties of what holds you back.

Lavender for calming anxiety.

Fennel encourages you to foresee the results of your intended actions.

COURAGE

Power Stone

Amethyst to activate the transformation of challenging situations.

Black tourmaline promotes confidence, diminishes fear and releases victim mentality.

Power Essence

Lemon assists with clarity and releasing limiting beliefs.

Jasmine boosts confidence and courage.

Lavender for calming anxiety.

PURPOSEFUL PRACTICALITIES

Power Stone

Tiger's eye provides you with the courage to stand up for yourself and implement boundaries.

Red jasper supports you during times of stress and strengthens your boundaries.

Power Essence

Ginger encourages courage and confidence. It improves willpower.

Rosemary acts as a protection from negative energy, keeping you strong in your boundaries and amplifies self-value and self-reliance.

Lavender for calming anxiety.

CAN-DO MOTIVATION

Power Stone

Carnelian is the stone of action that will give you courage and confidence to move forward on a new path. It also helps to clarify your goals and provides motivation.

Calcite calms the mind, creates emotional intelligence and assists in changing ideas into action.

Power Essence

Lemongrass is good for managing stress.

Peppermint moves you in the direction of where you need to go.

Patchouli helps you to see the bigger picture and feel emotionally safe.

Domestic Abuse Support Organisations

National Centre for Domestic Violence
www.ncdv.org.uk 0800 9702 070

Women's Aid
www.womensaid.org.uk 0808 2000 247

Refuge
www.refuge.org.uk 0808 2000 247

IDAS (Yorkshire)
www.idas.org.uk 0300 0110 110

Victim Support
www.victimsupport.org.uk 0808 1689 111

Citizens Advice Bureau
www.citizensadvice.org.uk

WomenCentre (W. Yorkshire)
www.womencentre.org.uk

Men's Advice Line
www.mensadviceline.org.uk 0808 801 0327

ManKind Initiative
www.mankind.org.uk 0182 3334 244

Honour Network
www.karmanirvana.org.uk 0800 599 9247

Galop LGBT Domestic Abuse Help
www.galop.org.uk 0800 9995 428

Montgomeryshire Family Crisis Centre
www.familycrisis.co.uk 0168 662 9114

National Stalking Helpline
www.stalkinghelpline.org 0808 802 0300

Next Steps?

You are invited to grow deeper and grow forward to Boldly Evolve, B.E.

For additional insights find out more at:

www.personalfreedommentor.com.

Here you will also be able to find out more about the D.A.R.E. 28-day workbook and Diana's unique online mentoring programme.

This online mentoring programme provides you with a personalised, fully-supported healing experience. The programme walks you through an inspiring/empowering process that supports you: helping you understand what you need to do to create your own unique freedom plan.

You will delve deeper into developing the necessary mindset and learn success strategies to access your own version of personal freedom.

If you want to create your own D.A.R.E. success story, discover more about how you could work with a personal freedom mentor to support and guide you through our online mentoring programme.

Get ready, DARE to B.E. you.

www.personalfreedommentor.com

Diana Onuma

Diana invites those who are yearning for freedom from toxic relationships to boldly evolve through practical support, mentoring and healing.

As a former barrister and family mediator Diana witnessed the traumatic effects of dysfunctional relationships on the personal and professional lives of her clients. This experience compelled Diana to start providing more practical, hands-on support to those who often feel trapped and alone.

Diana helps clients craft dynamic personal legacies that empower rather than perpetuate unhealthy patterns of silence, control and abuse. She brings together all her professional skills in order to encourage others to explore possibilities, speak up and move on with confidence and clarity through creativity, music and spirituality.

For those who want to move on from their current unhealthy relationships Diana offers workshops, retreats, online resources, one-to-one mentoring and ongoing support as they move to freedom.

FIND OUT MORE AT: www.personalfreedommentor.com

Other Books from mPowr Publishing

The Key: To Business & Pesonal Success

Martyn Pentecost

ISBN—978-1-907282-17-1

For those who are passionate about growing and developing. How to discover yourself and the most effective ways for you to flourish and enjoy success.

When Fish Climb Trees

Mel Liozou

ISBN— 978-1-907282-85-0

For those who are fed up of quick-fix solutions in the workplace and who want rich, productive relationships and results which flow from affirming values.

Invisible Me

Tyler Inman

ISBN— 978-1-907282-80-5

For those who want to understand what autism is all about, as told, in his own words, by a ten-year-old boy with Asperger's. Truly inspirational and challenging.

Speak Performance

Ges Ray

ISBN—978-1-907282-87-4

For those afraid of speaking in public, whether a huge crowd or in front of your team at work. How to be a confident, compelling and convincing speaker.

Other Books from DotDotDot Publishing

Unconscious Incarceration

Gethin Jones

ISBN—978-1-907282-86-7

For those trapped in cycles of addictive behaviour, desperate to find a way out. A personal account of freedom and a guide for your own journey.

Breathe With Ease

Alison Waring

ISBN—978-1-907282-88-1

For those looking for a powerful, natural approach to health. How to enable those with asthma and other breathing-related challenges to breathe with ease.

The Little Book of Holistic Accounting

Emma J Perry

ISBN—978-1-907282-81-2

For those stuck in a job or path that is stifling. How to balance the books of your body, mind, heart and soul.

Lightning Source UK Ltd.
Milton Keynes UK
UKHW011826280219
338223UK00003B/244/P